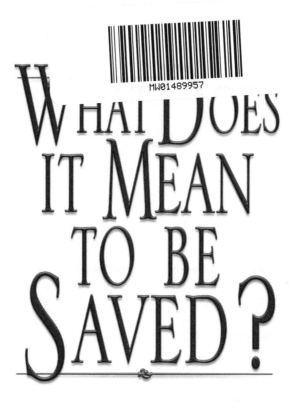

What Does It Mean to Be Saved?

Leslie Parrott

BEACON HILL PRESS
OF KANSAS CITY

ISBN 083-412-2464

Printed in the United States of America

Interior Design: Sharon Page

All Scripture quotations not otherwise designated are from the *New International Version®* (NIV®). Copyright © 1973, 1978, 1984 by International Bible Society. Used by permission of Zondervan Publishing House. All rights reserved.

Scripture marked NKJV is from the *New King James Version* (NKJV). Copyright © 1979, 1980, 1982 Thomas Nelson, Inc. Used by permission.

Scripture quotations marked KJV are from the King James Version of the Holy Bible.

10 9 8 7 6 5 4 3 2 1

Dedicated to the grandchildren
Lora Lee and I love so much:
Andrew and Justin
Grady and Madison
John and Jackson

CONTENTS

INTRODUCTION

This little book is one man's honest effort to explain salvation to three classes of people.

First, there are those who have heard the gospel so many times it is worn out, like an "old hat." They grew up in a family where the language of Canaan was the mother tongue. They attended Sunday School until their middle teens and then dropped out. In the meantime, they have learned to live without the church and without the lively presence of God. This little volume can be a map for the road back.

Second are those who have never been immersed in a satisfactory church experience. Their spiritual instincts are coming to life. They have found a group of Christian people they believe in. They need to become citizens in the kingdom of God on earth. They need to be born again.

And third, this material is prepared for people who "prayed through" long ago in an emotional experience they interpreted as conversion. Unfortunately, they have never understood what happened to them back there. They need to be able to give a reason for the faith they live by. I hope this book will be helpful.

The book opens with an overview of God, humanity, and salvation—the three topics under which the entire Bible can be organized. Next comes a working definition of sin and how it thrives in the hearts of men and women. If you can read but one chapter, I hope it will be chapter 5, "How Can I Be Saved?" It is both plain and practical, since it comes out of one man's personal experience with salvation.

I pray two prayers: Let this book lead someone to salvation. And second, let the scriptural basis of this material become the platform of faith from which people are able to give their own explanation of what it means to be saved.

1
GOD, HUMANITY, AND SALVATION

EVERYTHING BEGINS WITH GOD

In the beginning God created the heavens and the earth.
Now the earth was formless and empty,
darkness was over the surface of the deep,
and the Spirit of God was hovering over the waters.
And God said,
"Let there be light," and there was light.
Gen. 1:1-3

❋ ❋ ❋

THE CREATION OF HUMANITY

The LORD God formed the man
from the dust of the ground
and breathed into his nostrils the breath of life,
and the man became a living being. . . .
Then the LORD God made a woman from the rib
he had taken out of the man, and he brought her to the man.
2:7, 22

❋ ❋ ❋

THE FIRST SIGNPOST TO SALVATION

And I will put enmity
between you and the woman,
and between your offspring and hers;
he will crush your head,
and you will strike his heel.

3:15

❋ ❋ ❋

The Bible is the story of God, humanity, and salvation and how they relate to each other.

The Bible is also the saga of how God, humanity, and salvation have interacted over thousands of years past and will continue to be infinitely connected until the end of time.

First of All There Was God

No one can walk across the threshold of Genesis into the narrative of the Bible without facing the fact that God the Father Almighty created heaven and earth. He created the food chain and all forms of life that are sustained by it.

God organized the world into families through Abraham and his sons, grandsons, and great-grandsons. The extended families of Jacob became tribes under the leadership of 12 brothers. These 12 tribes were led by Moses out of Egypt. When they arrived in Judea, they began a very uncertain movement toward nationhood. The three most famous kings were Saul, David, and Solomon. Disintegration of the kingdom began as competition within David's family raised its ugly head and eventually resulted in two competing nations and the ultimate destruction of each.

After 70 years of captivity in what is now Iraq, the Jews came back to Jerusalem to rebuild their Temple and their city. But the kingdom was never the same again. The Roman emperors already had their eyes on the small strip of land—150 miles long and 65 miles wide—at the east end of the Mediterranean Sea. It was a central piece of real estate that offered the attractive possibility of increasing the Roman tax reserves substantially. But even in the worst of times, God had not abdicated. He was still deeply involved with people and their salvation.

Then There Was Humanity

God is the Universal Mind with supernatural power in His Word to create something out of nothing. The modern-day followers of Charles Darwin make a central issue over all life springing from a tiny, microscopic amoeba. But none of them has ever explained how something came from nothing. Where did the amoeba come from? This fact is now the most troublesome issue among scientists and philosophers who have explained the origins of life in terms of a life force or a big bang. God was and is that Source!

God's creative power is found in His *word*. A system of life was created out of the murky, amorphous darkness that engrossed the earth. "And the earth was without form, and void; and darkness was upon the face of the deep. And the Spirit of God moved upon the face of the waters" (Gen. 1:2, KJV). The powerful agent of creation was the spoken word of the Creator.

And God said,

Let there be light: and there was light. . . .

Let there be a firmament . . .

Let the waters under the heaven be gathered together unto one place, and let the dry land appear: and it was so. . . .

Let the earth bring forth grass . . .

Let there be lights in the firmament . . .
Let the waters bring forth abundantly . . .
Let the earth bring forth the living creature . . .
Let us make man in our image . . .

(vv. 3-26, KJV)

The word of God in creation is not a metaphor. It is not symbolism. The word continued to be the active agent of God throughout the entire Old Testament. God talked directly with Noah about his marine construction project. Heavenly messengers came to negotiate with Abraham about the destruction of Sodom. God spoke to Moses out of the burning bush. Each of the kings and prophets heard directly from God.

With the dawn of the New Testament, the Scripture says, "The Word was made flesh, and dwelt among us, (and we beheld his glory, the glory as of the only begotten of the Father,) full of grace and truth" (John 1:14, KJV).

Why God Created Humanity

Out of His goodness God wanted to share His love with someone who could love the way He loved. The animals and birds could not do this. His geographic systems such as light and dark, sun and rain, were magnificent to comprehend, but they could not form the deep loving relationship God desired. So God created creatures that could freely receive and return His love. The first man and woman were unlike anything else in creation. Not only could they share God's love with Him, but they could also share it with each other.

God would come down in the cool of the day to walk and talk with Adam and Eve. Can you imagine any better setting for deep, abiding fellowship than the three of them enjoyed with each other? It would be like us holding hands with someone we love while gazing into the ebbing embers of a fireplace in the place we call home. Or what could be more stimulating than a walk on the beach in the early morning with unhurried time to talk with the most important person in our life? This is the kind of relationship God had with Adam and Eve.

However, to prove their love, God gave the two mortals one prohibition. If they really loved Him, they were not to eat fruit from the "tree of knowledge." Satan planted bad ideas into the minds of Eve and Adam. He scandalized God by saying there was no way the Father could deliver on His words. Satan had a different philosophy. If it tasted good, why not partake? If the idea felt good, why not do it. Finally Adam and Eve, as it were, shook their clenched fists in the face of God and chose to have their own selfish will than to honor His love by obeying His single prohibition.

That evening, when God came down in the cool of the day to walk and talk with Adam and Eve, they were hiding, covering their nakedness, and thinking of excuses for their unacceptable behavior. Eve blamed the serpent. Adam blamed Eve, this "woman . . . thou gavest . . . me"! (Gen. 3:12, KJV).

The punishment was clear-cut. Adam and Eve no longer lived in unbroken fellowship with God. In some very important ways their relationship with each other was broken. They raised a dysfunctional family. They were separated from God and driven out of Eden. Adam had been created as the care provider for Eden, but now work became hard work, burdensome labor, exhausting, and only partially fulfilling. These factors of disobedience and punishment were passed on as moral characteristics within the human race. Humanity is in trouble. The human race needs help, now. The human race needs salvation, which only God gives through Christ our Lord.

The First Sign of Salvation

Humanity had only recently bought into the deceptions of Satan and given in to his temptations when the first small signpost appeared in the Garden of Eden pointing toward God's plan for salvation: "So the LORD God said to the serpent, 'Because you have done this . . . I will put enmity between you and the woman, and between your seed and her Seed; He shall bruise your head, and you shall bruise His heel'" (vv. 14-15, NKJV).

In the opening moments of Mel Gibson's film *The Passion of the Christ*, I nearly came out of my seat when Jesus, sitting on a boulder in Gethsemane, stomped on the head of the snake crawling toward Him. The bang was so loud and comprehensive, everyone in the audience gasped. My heart stood still—or so it seemed!

Between that promise from God in the Garden of Eden until the sword was driven through the side of Christ on the Cross, the atonement of God's love through His only Son Jesus runs like a mighty river in the Scriptures. It crescendos through the Resurrection events and fulfills itself in the coming of the Holy Spirit on the Day of Pentecost. The final fulfillment of Christ's glory and our salvation will occur in the Second Coming.

The Great Confession

Six weeks before Jesus was crucified, He withdrew with His disciples for a quiet time in the foothills of snowcapped Mount Hermon, near Damascus. It was here Peter made the great confession, "Thou art the Christ, the Son of the living God" (Matt. 16:16, KJV).

From that time on Jesus began to explain to his disciples that he must go to Jerusalem and suffer many things . . . that he must be killed and on the third day be raised to life.

Peter took him aside and began to rebuke him. "Never, Lord!" he said. "This shall never happen to you!"

Jesus turned and said to Peter, "Get behind me, Satan! You are a stumbling block to me; you do not have in mind the things of God, but the things of men."

Then Jesus said to his disciples, "If anyone would come after me, he must deny himself and take up his cross and follow me. For whoever wants to save his life will lose it, but whoever loses his life for me will find it (*Matt. 16:21-25*).

This magnificent passage makes clear the royal road to salvation is through the atonement of Christ. It also signifies the road people are to follow to salvation: (1) They must deny themselves. (2) They must take up their cross. (3) They must follow Christ. (4) They must lose their life in Christ.

God Through the Eyes of a Child

Joey is a precocious eight-year-old, in the west suburbs of Chicago, who drew his word picture of God in primary colors. He told me God was in charge of everything except the moms. They are in charge of themselves. According to Joey, God made everything and He keeps it all running as it's supposed to run, including such important things as the sun, moon, and stars. When God lets things break down for a little while, according to Joey, we have a storm. But God doesn't like storms, so most of the time everything works as it's supposed to.

I was surprised when Joey said one of God's biggest jobs was to keep enough people alive. God, he said, does this by making lots of babies. (Joey hasn't yet faced the challenge of overpopulation.) God knows there has got to be more people being born than dying. Otherwise, he said, the number of people on earth would get smaller and smaller.

Joey had an unusual idea about keeping the population balanced. God uses babies because they still have to grow up, and He doesn't have to face all the problems He would have if He started out with adults. His idea hit me so hard I began to wonder if the situation in the Garden of Eden might have turned out differently if God had created Adam and Eve as babies and not as full-blown adults.

I have an inward smile when I think of the precocious Joey. But I cannot help wondering how many unsaved adults are held back spiritually because of their own wrong concepts of God.

God is not a crotchety old man, easily angered and set in His ways. In fact, God is love! He is a "compassionate and gracious God, slow to anger, abounding in love and faithfulness" (Exod. 34:6).

Jesus is like His Father. If you want to know what God is like, read the Gospels. The picture of Jesus in these Gospels is the picture of the Father.

God is not a divine Person with both the desire and power to punish everyone who goes up against Him. God does not keep any scorecards. He is not interested in recording errors or keeping count of balls and strikes. With Him there are not winners and losers, only players—people who strike out, pop up, get on base, or hit the ball out of the park. But they are all His people. And He loves them, every one of them, from the batboy to the superstar.

Jesus' Ministry Was a Career in Three Years

Jesus invested the first year of His ministry in Galilee, where He became very popular through the impact of His miracles, especially for feeding the 5,000 men with the lunch of one boy. As a result, the people wanted to make Him king.

During the second year, Jesus concentrated on His teaching ministry, highlighting His compelling use of parables. These vivid stories Jesus told confounded His enemies and enthralled His followers. Both friend and foe were impressed. No one could ignore Jesus "because he taught as one who had authority, and not as their teachers of the law" (Matt. 7:29).

During His third year everything changed for Jesus. His popular following in Galilee faded measurably. The jealous anger of the Jewish leaders built to a crescendo. The report that Jesus had raised Lazarus from the dead—with witnesses to support the facts—sent the Sanhedrin into strategic planning sessions for His elimination. Several things happened to further their plans: (1) Jesus' kingly entrance into Jerusalem gave the rulers the seeds of an accusation they could use against Him with the Roman establishment. (2) His angry outburst in the commercial area of the Temple— overturning the money tables and lashing out with a whip —was blasphemy enough to call for a death sentence by this contingent of rulers who kept their jobs by repetitive proofs of their orthodoxy. (3) In a stroke of luck, an insider from Jesus' own company offered to turn Him in.

Knowing the end was at hand, Jesus made arrangements for a final meal with the disciples. Here, during an event that focused on how the Jews were saved out of Egypt, Jesus bared His soul: (1) He washed and dried their feet in a teaching sacrament of humility. (2) He told them about His departure, which was at hand. He would be going to His Father's house although He would eventually return for them. (3) He set up the guidelines of a memorial meal they could repeat until His return. (4) He made it clear He would die and be buried but would also rise again on the third day. (5) He dealt with His absence by clarifying who would take His place, the Comforter, whom most of us know as the Holy Spirit. (6) At this point, they sang a hymn and went from the dining table to the Garden of Gethsemane.

Thus the mature follower of Jesus finds the way of salvation through (1) the Holy Spirit who is the Representative of Christ on earth and the Implementer of the Word of God among us; (2) by the finished atonement of Jesus Christ on the Cross and in the power of His resurrection; and, finally, (3) by divine grace provided by God the Father Almighty.

The Triune God works as one in providing the cure for the sin-sick soul of a person, tormented by the shame of his or her spiritual condition and wracked with guilt because of his or her depraved inability to hit the right mark consistently.

Thus with this biblical backdrop we are ready now to move from "God, humanity, and salvation" to the next fundamental question, "What is sin?"

Talking Points

- Isn't it strange how people can trash God, profane Christ, ignore the Holy Spirit, and then wonder why the world is going to hell?
- Isn't it strange how people can say they believe in God and then run their lives as if He didn't even exist?
- It isn't enough to believe that God exists; some of the worst kinds of sinners believe God exists. "You believe that there is one God. Good! Even the demons believe that—and shudder" (James 2:19).

2
WHAT IS SIN?

TEMPTATION AND SIN

But each one is tempted when,
by his own evil desire,
he is dragged away and enticed.
Then, after desire has conceived,
it gives birth to sin;
and sin,
when it is full-grown, gives birth to death.
James 1:14-15

❋ ❋ ❋

TAKING AWAY OUR SINS

But you know that he appeared
so that he might take away our sins.
And in him is no sin.
No one who lives in him keeps on sinning.
No one who continues to sin has either seen him or known him.
1 John 3:5-6

❋ ❋ ❋

Time is the most precious of all human possessions.

Time is both fragile and limited. Time, like old-growth timber or pools of oil in the heart of the earth, cannot be renewed. When they are gone, they're gone!

Love and Time

In an effort to generate more time, we develop enter-prising approaches for extracting it from relationships. These relationships are like the root systems that support the big trees in Sequoia National Park. For instance, we try to redeem lost time by redefining the small amounts of it we spend with our children as "high-quality time." We ig-nore our spouses and think they will understand. We throw our weight around, expecting people to ignore that they are being coerced and to keep on cooperating without a show of irritation. It takes additional time to work with people, talk things out with our husbands or wives, or lis-ten to our children. Dictators get things done faster. But re-lationships only grow when people partner rather than dominate.

In church we tilt our hat to God with a tip instead of a tithe. We sit in the stands and never hesitate to hoot at the mistakes of those who play the game. In fact, some church-goers profess faith but live as if God did not exist. The most critical sin that alienates us from God faster than any other is stubborn unwillingness or the inability to give God enough time for our relationship to work.

Some people all but post a sign on the door of their heart that reads, "No Time for God!" We have not learned that being saved is a relationship. And good relationships take time. The most significant gift you can present to someone you love is a generous segment of your time. In the God-human relationship God is always available, but too often, we are not.

Since time for God competes with the fun sin offers, the balance between time for God and time for sinful pleasures is weighted heavily in favor of sin. Not everyone has the good judgment of Moses: "By faith Moses . . . chose to be mistreated along with the people of God rather than to enjoy the pleasures of sin for a short time" (Heb. 11:24-25).

Because time is our most precious possession, many try to work out a satisfactory spiritual life that confines God to clearly defined times and spaces. We don't want to give Him any more of ourselves—meaning our time—than is necessary to answer the question, "How little religion can I have and still get to heaven?"

On any given Sunday morning, about half of America shows up in church. Many must feel the precious hour they spend on a padded pew, facing the Cross and the pulpit, is about all God needs from them in the space of a week. As one lady said to me regarding her exposure to the means of grace, "A little dab will do you!"

On the other hand, we like God to be available 24/7. We need Him on call when we hurt, when we are sick or at funerals, and all other times that call for strength from beyond ourselves. We want God to be on hand when our babies are baptized or our sons and daughters are married. We expect God to reward us for praying. This "divine gift-giver" needs to know there are just some things we can't live without. Therefore He must provide them. That is His job.

Many people never think of needing God during times of work and play. That's our time. We own it. It belongs to us. We use it as we see fit. It is a given that we are in control. Besides that, we presume God is not interested in the daily lives of His creation. That is an easy out. So unless we run into trouble, our relationship with God runs on two *on-again, off-again*, alternating pistons.

But for the person who knows what it means to be saved, there are no times or spaces off limits to God. There are no personal time blocks closed to His abiding presence. For the saved man or woman, walking and talking with

God in the cool of the day is as restorative now as it was for Adam and Eve before their calamitous fall.

The Character of a Happy Man

The happiest man in the Book of Psalms is described in a few successive statements that open the book. This "blessed (or happy) man" chose (1) whom he walked with, (2) whom he loitered with, and (3) whose welcome mat he never crossed. (4) He rejoiced in knowing and keeping God's law. (5) He was as solid as a tree. (6) All his enterprises prospered.

Blessed is the man
Who walks not in the counsel of the ungodly,
Nor stands in the path of sinners,
Nor sits in the seat of the scornful;
But his delight is in the law of the LORD,
And in His law he meditates day and night.
He shall be like a tree
Planted by the rivers of water,
That brings forth its fruit in its season,
Whose leaf also shall not wither;
And whatever he does shall prosper.
—*Ps. 1:1-3*, NKJV

Since sin is separation from God because of (1) rejection, (2) disobedience, or (3) disinterest, we need to understand the many ways sin expresses itself. Sin as depravity or lifestyle has many faces. Here are a few:

Sin Is Moral Corruption Activated by Lust

Peter wrote, "Whereby are given unto us exceeding great and precious promises: that by these ye might be partakers of the divine nature, having escaped the corruption that is in the world through lust" (2 Pet 1:4, KJV).

Jesus had two things in mind when He warned that examining a woman with bedroom eyes was equivalent to committing adultery (see Matt. 5:28): (1) Sin occurs in the heart before it moves to the eyes, feet, hands, or other action centers of the body. (2) The willful act of fornication or adultery is a matter of *coulda—woulda—shoulda*—not a God-given appreciation for a well-formed body.

Sin begins with intention: I would if I could. Sin is certainly more than an involuntary desire. An adulterous man capitulates in the inner man, and from there forward, adultery is simply a matter of opportunity. As James 1:14-15 says, "Each one is tempted when, by his own evil desire, he is dragged away and enticed. Then, after desire has conceived, it gives birth to sin; and sin, when it is full-grown, gives birth to death."

John Defines Sin in Terms of Law and Will

In his first letter, John set forth the essential character of sin as (1) breaking of the law, (2) rejecting God's will and purpose, and (3) the substitution of self-will for the will of God. He said, "Everyone who sins breaks the law; in fact, sin is lawlessness" (1 John 3:4).

Sin is not unbelief that stems from ignorance but is an attitude or a behavior pattern that results from rejection. If desire is operative, feeling turns into sin when hands touch, eyes meet, or feet move toward each other.

John saw sin as an aggressive possibility but not as an absolute necessity: "But you know that he appeared so that he might take away our sins. And in him is no sin. No one who lives in him keeps on sinning. No one who continues to sin has either seen him or known him" (1 John 3:5-6).

John nailed down his argument on sin as lawlessness with one final statement:

He who does what is sinful is of the devil, because the devil has been sinning from the beginning. The reason the Son of God appeared was to destroy the devil's work. No one who is born of God will continue to sin, because God's seed remain in him; he cannot go on sinning, because he has been born of God. This is how we know who the children of God are and who the children of the devil are: Anyone who does not do what is right is not a child of God; nor is anyone who does not love his brother (vv. 8-10).

Berkhof, a well-known Calvinist theologian, wrote in his *Systematic Theology* (Berkhof, 231) that sin "is not something passive, such as a weakness, a fault or an imperfection for which we cannot be held responsible, but an active opposition to God, and a positive transgression of his law which constitutes guilt. Sin is the result of a free but evil choice of man."

The Consequences of Sin Are Not Negotiable

The opening line in Richard Taylor's 1945 book *A Right Concept of Sin* is, "Sin, as one doctrine of the Christian system, is the common denominator of the other doctrines" (Taylor, 9). He believes the doctrines on sin constitute the core around which all the other Christian doctrines are built.

H. V. Miller in "The Sin Problem" (quoted by Taylor, 11) says, "The sin question is the pivotal question. Anything taught or preached that obscures the cruciality of sin is an enemy of the Cross."

Jesus was unequivocal toward sin: "He [God] cuts off every branch in me that bears no fruit, while every branch that does bear fruit he prunes [encourages] so that it will be even more fruitful" (John 15:2).

The nonnegotiable character of sin and its consequences is claimed in many scriptural passages. Here are a few:

- "The soul who sins is the one who will die" (Ezek. 18:4).
- Paul was grappling with this nonnegotiable fact of sin when he wrote of himself, "I know that nothing good lives in me, that is, in my sinful nature. For I have the desire to do what is good, but I cannot carry it out" (Rom. 7:18).
- "For the wages of sin is death" (6:23).
- "As for you, you were dead in your transgressions and sins" (Eph. 2:1).
- "Then, after desire has conceived, it gives birth to sin; and sin, when it is full-grown, gives birth to death" (James 1:15).

Sin Generates a Heavy Burden of Guilt

During a game in Ameriquest Field in Arlington, Texas, a high, hard-hit foul ball landed at the feet of a 4-year-old boy in the third-base stands. However, an overly zealous 28-year-old fan, sitting behind the boy, knocked him against the seats and grabbed the ball for himself. An angry mother struck the man with her rolled up newspaper, while the fans chanted, "Give the boy the ball." But he refused!

Reggie Sanders, a Cardinal outfielder who witnessed the scroungy event, went into the stands and gave the little boy, Nicholas Obrian, a bat. Nolan Ryan, from the Texas Rangers, presented Nick an autographed ball.

What happened was shown on television across the nation. And the mother, who appeared with Nick on *Good Morning America*, admitted calling Mr. Starr a jerk, among other names. She said, "You trampled a 4-year-old boy to get this ball." He replied, "Oh, well!"

Four days later, after growing weary from a heavy bur-den of guilt, Mr. Starr, who was a former youth minister in a nearby church, announced his plan. He did not say he was doing these things to alleviate the heavy personal guilt he bore. But nonetheless he was. The guilt was (1) strictly personal, (2) heavier than he expected, and (3) endured longer than he wished. He needed a cure.

Mr. Starr wrote a letter of apology, gave the ball to the boy, and bought tickets for Nick and his entire family for a Texas Rangers game. Guilt has a way of imposing itself on a person in a heavy load that is powerful, personal, and per-severing.

Sin Is a Universal Problem

The Bible, the morning newspapers, and what we see in our private worlds, including television, testify to one reali-ty—sin is universal.

The narratives of the Old Testament are often tedious in the unending revelation of violence and disobedience involving the Israelites. During the long years between Moses and David, the recorded times of faith and loyalty to God are irregular and spasmodic.

Jesus on Sin

Jesus identified the home of sin to be in the inner man, the soul, or the heart. All these words—"inner man," "soul," and "heart"—are synonymous. They are the home where sin is cultivated. "For out of the heart come evil thoughts" (Matt. 15:19).

Jesus also made sin easy to identify. Every sinful act be-gins as an evil thought in the mind. Then as opportunity nods its head toward the home of evil, thoughts become gross sins, like "murder, adultery, sexual immorality, theft, false testimony, slander" (v. 19).

Paul on Sin

In the first chapter of Paul's important letter to the Christians in Rome, Paul identifies sin in no uncertain terms:

Furthermore, since they did not think it worthwhile to retain the knowledge of God, he gave them over to a depraved mind, to do what ought not to be done. They have become filled with every kind of wickedness, evil, greed and depravity. They are full of envy, murder, strife, deceit and malice. They are gossips, slanderers, God-haters, insolent, arrogant and boastful; they invent ways of doing evil; they disobey their parents; they are senseless, faithless, heartless, ruthless. Although they know God's righteous decree that those who do such things deserve death, they not only continue to do these very things but also approve of those who practice them (1:28-32).

Who can read Galatians and not recognize sin as a fact of life?

The acts of the sinful nature are obvious: sexual immorality, impurity and debauchery; idolatry and witchcraft; hatred, discord, jealousy, fits of rage, selfish ambition, dissensions, factions and envy; drunkenness, orgies, and the like. I warn you, as I did before, that those who live like this will not inherit the kingdom of God (5:19-21).

Even in Paul's letter to the Ephesians, which is a beautiful description of the church, sin is still described explicitly:

Therefore each of you must put off falsehood and speak truthfully to his neighbor, for we are all members of one body. "In your anger do not sin": Do not let the sun go down while you are still angry, and do not give the devil a foothold. He who has been stealing must steal no longer, but must work, doing something useful with his own hands, that he may have something to share with those in need. Do not let any unwholesome talk come out of your mouths, but only what is helpful for building others up according to their needs, that it may benefit those who listen *(4:25-29)*.

The Colossians, who by the record were sweet-spirited believers, got their share of the sin message from Paul:

> Put to death, therefore, whatever belongs to your earthly nature: sexual immorality, impurity, lust, evil desires and greed, which is idolatry. Because of these, the wrath of God is coming. You used to walk in these ways, in the life you once lived. But now you must rid yourselves of all such things as these: anger, rage, malice, slander, and filthy language from your lips. Do not lie to each other, since you have taken off your old self with its practices *(3:5-9)*.

If Paul dealt forthrightly with the issue of sin in each of his major letters to the churches, we can expect him to face the issue straight on in a letter to his young protégé, Timothy. Paul saw this youth leader's ministry too valuable for any risk of confusion concerning sin.

> We also know that law is made not for the righteous but for lawbreakers and rebels, the ungodly and sinful, the unholy and irreligious; for those who kill their fathers or mothers, for murderers, for adulterers and perverts, for slave traders and liars and perjurers—and for whatever else is contrary to the sound doctrine that conforms to the glorious gospel of the blessed God, which he entrusted to me *(1 Tim. 1:9-11)*.

Moses and the Ten Commandments

All the law there is in the Bible finally funnels back to the commandments God gave Moses on Mount Sinai.

These are not just rules but great principles of attitude and behavior that, at their core, are principles of right and wrong. The first four commandments focus on our relationship with God, and the other six, on our relationships with each other, beginning with the family.

There is a parable concerning a summit to save the world from blowing itself up. All the wisdom of the ages was entered into a super gigantic computer to determine what great wisdom existed that could save the world from ultimate destruction. Everything the philosophers, poets, theologians, historians, fiction writers, and other people with spiritual and human insight had procured was entered into this one-of-a-kind computer. When the "play" button was finally pushed, the words printed out on the screen were the following:

And God spoke all these words: . . .

You shall have no other gods before me.

You shall not make for yourself an idol. . . .

You shall not misuse the name of the LORD your God. . . .

Remember the Sabbath day by keeping it holy. . . .

Honor your father and your mother, so that you may live long. . . .

You shall not murder.

You shall not commit adultery.

You shall not steal.

You shall not give false testimony. . . .

You shall not covet . . . anything that belongs to your neighbor.

(Exod. 20:1, 3-4, 7-8, 12-17)

The purpose of the Ten Commandments is (1) to build into humanity's inner self a strong feeling of God consciousness:

Then the LORD came down in the cloud and stood there with him and proclaimed his name, the LORD. And he passed in front of Moses, proclaiming, "The LORD, the LORD, the compassionate and gracious God, slow to anger, abounding in love and faithfulness, maintaining love to thousands, and forgiving wickedness, rebellion and sin. Yet he does not leave the guilty unpunished; he punishes the children and their children for the sin of the fathers to the third and fourth generation" (34:5-7).

The purpose of the Ten Commandments is (2) to build within humanity's inner nature a strong sense of sin consciousness.

- "Therefore no one will be declared righteous in his sight by observing the law; rather, through the law we become conscious of sin" (Rom. 3:20).
- "The law was added so that the trespass might increase. But where sin increased, grace increased all the more" (5:20).
- "All who rely on observing the law are under a curse, for it is written: 'Cursed is everyone who does not continue to do everything written in the Book of the Law'" (Gal. 3:10).

The purpose of the Ten Commandments is (3) to create in humanity's inner nature a strong need for a Savior.

Before this faith came, we were held prisoners by the law, locked up until faith should be revealed. So the law was put in charge to lead us to Christ that we might be justified by faith (vv. 23-24).

There are two things the Ten Commandments cannot do: (1) keeping them does not save a person from sin, and (2) keeping them does not change a person's nature. Redemption, adoption, justification, and sanctification are not effected by the Law, even when it is kept meticulously:

- "Through him [Christ] everyone who believes is justified from everything you could not be justified from by the law of Moses" (Acts 13:39).
- "Clearly no one is justified before God by the law, because, 'The righteous will live by faith'" (Gal. 3:11).
- "(For the law made nothing perfect), and a better hope is introduced, by which we draw near to God" (Heb. 7:19).
- "This is an illustration for the present time, indicating that the gifts and sacrifices being offered were not able to clear the conscience of the worshiper. They are only a matter of food and drink and various ceremonial washings—external regulations applying until the time of the new order" (9:9-10).

Christ became the sacrifice for sin, once for all:

The law is only a shadow of the good things that are coming—not the realities themselves. For this reason it can never, by the same sacrifices repeated endlessly year after year, make perfect those who draw near to worship. If it could, would they not have stopped being offered? For the worshipers would have been cleansed once for all, and would no longer have felt guilty for their sins. But those sacrifices are an annual reminder of sins, because it is impossible for the blood of bulls and goats to take away sins. Therefore, when Christ came into the world, he said: "Sacrifice and offering you did not desire, but a body you prepared for me" (10:1-5).

The Greatest Commandment of All

Hearing that Jesus had silenced the Sadducees, the Pharisees got together. One of them, an expert in the law, tested him with this question: "Teacher, which is the greatest commandment in the Law?" Jesus replied: "'Love the Lord your God with all your heart and with all your soul and with all your mind.' This is the first and greatest commandment. And the second is like it: 'Love your neighbor as yourself.' All the Law and the Prophets hang on these two commandments" (Matt. 22:34-40).

The summary of all the Law given in the Scriptures is organized in three centers.

- We must love God—Father, Son, and Holy Spirit—with all our might.
- We must cultivate love for our neighbors—in general and specifically. This is agape love, the same kind God has. This love does not depend on reciprocation or even emotion. Agape love is a decision to affirm all the people in our private world, just as they are and not the way we wish they were.
- Finally, we need an adequate, functioning level of self-acceptance. We all experience guilt, because it comes from every careless thing we do or say. It may be (1) self-imposed guilt that comes from falling below our own standard. Or it may be (2) divine guilt that generates godly sorrow within us and calls for repentance. But either way, guilt always calls for an adequate remedy.

I have always felt Billy Graham chose an inspired title for his autobiography *Just As I Am*. I wish I were smarter, more understanding, wiser, and more experienced. That would make me a better person. But the fact is I must (1) accept myself just as I am, (2) present myself fully to Christ as the Lord of my life, and (3) emulate the values of Jesus in my lifestyle. Jesus said, "I am the way and the truth and the life" (John 14:6).

An anchor on NBC's *Nightly News* reported the need of 4,300 people in the United States for heart transplants. Last year, half that number received them. Deaths for lack of the transplants occurred to 25 percent of the needy just because they did not have the physical strength to wait out the snail-paced line to the operating room.

In a second segment of this same report, the NBC people contrasted the despair among those who had lost hope and the joyous ecstasy among those who received the gift of a new life. Those two news reports are a good metaphor for what happens among sinners, with one dramatic difference—God has a transplant for each and every guilty sinner. No sinner needs to lose hope, for Jesus said, "Let not your heart be troubled: ye believe in God, believe also in me" (John 14:1, KJV). He also said, "Come to me, all you who are weary and burdened, and I will give you rest. Take my yoke upon you and learn from me, for I am gentle and humble in heart, and you will find rest for your souls. For my yoke is easy and my burden is light" (Matt. 11:28-30).

After this rather long discussion on "What is sin?" we are ready now for the next chapter, "Power in the Blood."

Talking Points

- What is temptation and how does it come alive?
- What can you do to generate more time for your relationships, including your relationship with God?
- How can you give God more time?
- What makes sin enjoyable?
- According to the first psalm, what are the decisions made by a happy man?
- What is sin?

3

POWER IN THE BLOOD

CHRIST AS A SACRIFICE

God presented him as a sacrifice of atonement,
through faith in his blood.
He did this to demonstrate his justice,
because in his forbearance
he had left the sins committed beforehand unpunished—
he did it to demonstrate his justice at the present time,
so as to be just and the one who justifies
those who have faith in Jesus.
Rom. 3:25-26

❋ ❋ ❋

THE STAIN OF GUILT

There is a fountain filled with blood
Drawn from Immanuel's veins;
And sinners, plunged beneath that flood,
Lose all their guilty stains.
William Cowper, 1731—1800

❋ ❋ ❋

The designation of our Savior as the "Lord Jesus Christ" is a revelation of precisely who He is. "Jesus" is the name given Him by Mary and Joseph. "Christ" is the title for Messiah. And "Lord" is the relationship a believer may enjoy with Him.

Jesus Christ is (1) God's only Son, (2) born of a virgin, (3) the central figure of human history, (4) provider of salvation, (5) founder of the Christian Church, and (6) High Priest seated at God's right hand, (7) from whence He will come to judge the living and the dead.

Birth and Upbringing

Jesus was born in Bethlehem, only a few miles south of Jerusalem. His birth came near the end of the reign of Herod the Great, who was appointed governor and commissioned by Rome to keep peace among the Jews. He tried to placate them with a new Temple but ruled with the iron hand of a despot from 37 B.C. to A.D. 4. Spooked by the magi's word about the birth of a king, Herod ordered the slaughter of the toddlers. With a warning from the angel Gabriel and financial support from the gifts of gold, frankincense, and myrrh, the holy family moved to Egypt, where Jesus lived as a small boy. After Herod died, the family returned to Israel and settled in Nazareth. Jesus grew up in a devout Jewish home in a town overlooking the highway that linked Damascus with Mediterranean coastal cities and the mysterious land of Egypt. They were rural, small-town people. Jesus played games, climbed trees, and fished in the Sea of Galilee, where He would later preach, teach, and do His miracles.

The Ministry of Jesus

In A.D. 27 or 28, Jesus sought baptism in the lower Jordan River, at the hands of His cousin John. Jesus was glorified by "the Spirit like a dove descending upon him: and there came a voice from heaven, saying, Thou art my beloved Son, in whom I am well pleased" (Mark 1:10-11, KJV).

After His baptism, Jesus was led by the Spirit into the desert, where the temptations about His mission were as severe as the devil could make them (v. 13). The third big event in the beginning of His ministry was the return of Jesus from the desert to Galilee, where He preached the gospel of the kingdom of God (v. 15). He stayed on message to the end of His ministry, which included the 40 days after the Resurrection. He taught His disciples to pray, "Thy kingdom come. Thy will be done in earth, as it is in heaven" (Matt. 6:10, KJV).

The ministry of Jesus can be divided roughly by the focus of His time and energies. The first year was a time of teaching about the Kingdom. (1) This included such things as the Sermon on the Mount and the introduction of the parables as a favorite tool in Jesus' teaching kit. (2) The second year was an era of popularity. This peak time closed with the feeding of the 5,000 men, which resulted in the throngs wanting Him for their king. (3) The third year was a natural follow-up on the first two. The enormous popularity of Jesus aroused the jealousy and anger of the Jewish hierarchy, who began their strategies for getting rid of Him. This was His year of rejection, which ended with death on the Cross.

Although the Gospel record of Christ's teachings and miracles is important, the most space in the four Gospels is given to the passion of our Lord. Jesus was (1) rejected by the Jewish hierarchy, (2) condemned by Herod, (3) crucified by the Romans, (4) confined in a borrowed tomb, (5) confirmed by His resurrection to new life, and (6) crowned king at the right hand of the throne of His Father, from whence He will come to judge the living and the dead.

Offering Jesus as the Atonement for Sin Was the Father's Idea

Any discussion of the Atonement must begin with God, a fact made abundantly clear in the New Testament. For instance, the "golden text" of the Bible begins with God's love. That same love is the Father's motivation for giving His Son as the change agent for eternal change from death to life. "For God so loved the world that he gave his one and only Son, that whoever believes in him shall not perish but have eternal life" (John 3:16).

Humanity did not do anything to deserve the atonement the Father provided in His Son's death on the Cross. Sinners do not deserve atonement, but God provides it anyway. "But God demonstrates his own love for us in this: While we were still sinners, Christ died for us" (Rom. 5:8).

The purpose of Christ's death was not to reconcile an angry God to undeserving men and women. It was men and women that needed reconciliation, not God. In a strange way none of us can fully understand, the Father reconciled us to himself through the death of His Son. Because Paul believed that God demonstrated His love to the human race through Christ's death and resurrection, he became a strong advocate for reconciliation. "God was reconciling the world to himself in Christ, not counting men's sins against them. And he has committed to us the message of reconciliation" (2 Cor. 5:19).

Christ's Death Is a Judgment Against Sin

Mind, emotions, and will are the three components that constitute the inner self, that part of a person that will live forever. Each of these three factors undergoes change through the power of the Spirit: (1) *The will*, which is naturally devoted to carnal purposes, can be cleansed and focused on the values of Christ. (2) *The negative emotions*, such as out-of-control anger, can be infused with the spirit of Christian love, a move that changes how we feel about everything. (3) *And the mind*, which is the center of the decision-making process, can be changed from a center of hostility toward both God and others, to a place of life and peace.

- "The mind of sinful man is death, but the mind controlled by the Spirit is life and peace; the sinful mind is hostile to God. It does not submit to God's law, nor can it do so. Those controlled by the sinful nature cannot please God. You, however, are controlled not by the sinful nature but by the Spirit, if the Spirit of God lives in you" (Rom. 8:6-9).

- "Who gave himself for us to redeem us from all wickedness and to purify for himself a people that are his very own, eager to do what is good" (Titus 2:14).

- "For what the law was powerless to do in that it was weakened by the sinful nature, God did by sending his own Son in the likeness of sinful man to be a sin offering. And so he condemned sin in sinful man" (Rom. 8:3).

Christ's Death Demonstrates God's Wrath Against Sin

There is no doubt the Cross was a tangible expression of the attitude of God toward sin. What happened on the Cross demonstrates the attitude of God's *love* for sinners and God's *wrath* against sin. The word "wrath" is a strong New Testament term that expresses the divine reaction to sin.

"Let no one deceive you with empty words, for . . . God's wrath comes on those who are disobedient" (Eph. 5:6).

Christ will not always reveal His love toward sinners.

His patience will run thin. Probation is not forever. And when the love of God turns to "the wrath of the Lamb," there will no longer be a meek and mild Jesus allowing His enemies to spit in His face. Wearing the robes of an eternal judge, He will pour out the vials of divine wrath on all those who have rejected His offer of loving forgiveness for their sins.

"They called to the mountains and the rocks, 'Fall on us and hide us from the face of him who sits on the throne and from the wrath of the Lamb!'" (Rev. 6:16).

The most extensive expression of the wrath of God comes in the opening of Romans, where Paul characterized the condition of obstreperous, vile, disobedient humanity. Three times Paul says that "God gave them up" to be absorbed in the sin-ravaged ways they had already chosen for themselves. There is a drumbeat of dread in these words: "God gave them over in the sinful desires of their hearts. . . . God gave them over to shameful lusts. . . . he [God] gave them over to a depraved mind" (Rom. 1:24, 26, 28).

Christ's Death Is a Sacrifice on His Part for Our Sins

Jesus was not forced to die on a cross. He was not crucified as a helpless victim. The Jews accused Him before Pilate, who used his Roman authority—against the best judgment of his wife—to order the crucifixion of Jesus. But, in spite of the Jews and the Romans, Jesus could have called 10,000 angels to fight His battle. But He died alone! He chose to become the sacrifice of our atonement. Numerous scriptures bear out this connection:

- "God presented him as a sacrifice of atonement, through faith in his blood. He did this to demonstrate his justice, because in his forbearance he had left the sins committed beforehand unpunished—he did it to demonstrate his justice at the present time, so as to be just and the one who justifies those who have faith in Jesus" (Rom. 3:25-26).

- "For Christ's love compels us, because we are convinced that one died for all, and therefore all died. And he died for all, that those who live should no longer live for themselves but for him who died for them and was raised again. . . . God made him who had no sin to be sin for us, so that in him we might become the righteousness of God" (2 Cor. 5:14-15, 21).

- "For you know that it was not with perishable things such as silver or gold that you were redeemed from the empty way of life handed down to you from your forefathers, but with the precious blood of Christ, a lamb without blemish or defect. He was chosen before the creation of the world, but was revealed in these last times for your sake. Through him you believe in God, who raised him from the dead and glorified him, and so your faith and hope are in God" (1 Pet. 1:18-21).

The Death of Christ Was a Vicarious Deed

Not only was the cross of Christ a *judgment upon sin*, but it was also a *vicarious act* on the part of Christ. "Vicarious" is a word that literally means *substitute*, but it can also refer to a representative who acts on behalf of another. So in a vicarious death, it is possible for one person not only to take the place of others but also to represent them. The biblical idea of corporate personality is present here. This is the understanding that an entire group can be summed up in one individual. Whatever the individual experiences as the group's representative, the group experiences as well, and vice versa. In this way Christ identified with our humanity and represented us to God and also represented God to us. He bridged the gap that separated us from God. So when Christ died on behalf of us, we all shared in His suffering and death, and through faith in Him find forgiveness and reconciliation with God. He was the representational substitute for every man and woman, past, present, and future.

"For even the Son of Man did not come to be served, but to serve, and to give his life as a ransom for many" (Mark 10:45).

One of the great Old Testament passages on the vicarious death of Jesus comes from the inspired pen of Isaiah:

"But he was pierced for our transgressions, he was crushed for our iniquities; the punishment that brought us peace was upon him, and by his wounds we are healed. We all, like sheep, have gone astray, each of us has turned to his own way; and the LORD has laid on him the iniquity of us all" (Isa. 53:5-6).

The Sacrificial Death of Jesus Is More Easily Accepted than Explained

The idea of sacrifice pervades every segment of the New Testament. Jesus initiated the explanation of His death as a sacrifice based on the idea of sacrifice found in Isa. 53. He anticipated the sacrifice of His life for others.

"I tell you the truth, unless a kernel of wheat falls to the ground and dies, it remains only a single seed. But if it dies, it produces many seeds. The man who loves his life will lose it, while the man who hates his life in this world will keep it for eternal life" (John 12:24-25).

The Lord's Supper contains sacrificial terms that were practices in the Old Testament. From the time God first taught Jews how to worship, blood was a significant symbol. The fact that life is in the blood was taught by Moses. When the sacrifice was slain, the blood of the animal was offered to God to represent the person making the sacrifice. The best known maxim on the power of the blood is recorded in Heb. 9:22: "Without the shedding of blood there is no forgiveness."

"For the life of a creature is in the blood, and I have given it to you to make atonement for yourselves on the altar; it is the blood that makes atonement for one's life" (Lev. 17:11).

This same metaphor of the blood was used by Jesus in the ritual He introduced for the Lord's Supper in the Upper Room. From then until now, followers of Christ (disciples) have recited what Jesus taught them to say and have meditated on the purpose of the body and the blood:

> While they were eating, Jesus took bread, gave thanks and broke it, and gave it to his disciples, saying, "Take it; this is my body." Then he took the cup, gave thanks and offered it to them, and they all drank from it. "This is my blood of the covenant, which is poured out for many," he said to them. "I tell you the truth, I will not drink again of the fruit of the vine until that day when I drink it anew in the kingdom of God" (Mark 14:22-25).

Paul was fully focused on the blood atonement when he wrote the strong passage on the Lord's Supper in his first letter to the Corinthians. It is a long passage, but well worth reading.

> For I received from the Lord what I also passed on to you: The Lord Jesus, on the night he was betrayed, took bread, and when he had given thanks, he broke it and said, "This is my body, which is for you; do this in remembrance of me." In the same way, after supper he

took the cup, saying, "This cup is the new covenant in my blood; do this, whenever you drink it, in remembrance of me." For whenever you eat this bread and drink this cup, you proclaim the Lord's death until he comes.

Therefore, whoever eats the bread or drinks the cup of the Lord in an unworthy manner will be guilty of sinning against the body and blood of the Lord. A man ought to examine himself before he eats of the bread and drinks of the cup. For anyone who eats and drinks without recognizing the body of the Lord eats and drinks judgment on himself *(11:23-29)*.

After discussion of the efficacious blood of Jesus, the next chapter, "The Lamb Won!" is a natural follow-up.

Talking Points

- In the Atonement, why is blood so important?
- What are the six unique characteristics of Jesus and what do they mean?
- What were the significant happenings in the baptism of Jesus?
- Why did the atonement of Christ begin with the Father?
- In what way is the death of Christ a judgment against sin?

4

THE LAMB WON!

WHO IS THE LAMB?

The next day John saw Jesus coming toward him and said,
"Look, the Lamb of God,
who takes away the sin of the world!" . . .
Then John gave this testimony:
"I saw the Spirit come down from heaven as a dove
and remain on him.
I would not have known him,
except that the one who sent me to baptize with water told me,
'The man on whom you see the Spirit come down and remain
is he who will baptize with the Holy Spirit.'
I have seen and I testify that this is the Son of God."
The next day John was standing there with two of his disciples.
. . . he said,
"Look, the Lamb of God!"
John 1:29, 32-36

❋ ❋ ❋

If it is possible for a man to be groomed for meanness from childhood it was Nicolae Ceauşescu, the despotic ruler of Romania from 1968 until 1989. When he arrived in Bucharest as an 11-year-old apprentice to a shoemaker, trouble came with him. While walking through the railroad station, he stole a piece of luggage. When he was arrested by the police, it turned out to be a valise full of unlawful Communist flyers. Assuming he was a Communist, the police put him in jail with some of socialism's most radical advocates. At 15 years of age he was arrested for agitating a strike. He was arrested again the next year for collecting signatures protesting the trial of railway workers. He tried to go underground but was arrested again at 18 years of age and locked up in the infamous Doftana Prison for two years. Each of these lockups was like another segment in an advanced degree program in mean behavior for use in molding defenseless people to fit a Communist vision of things.

When he became ruler of Romania, Ceaușescu inaugurated plans for the urbanization of the country. He began demolishing entire villages, moving the people against their will into large block apartment houses near the center of Bucharest. To him, the feelings of the country people were null and void. They simply did not matter to him. All that mattered was his "urbanization" and "industrialization" programs. To achieve these purposes the secret police maintained firm control over free speech wherever it was heard.

Ceaușescu's harshest vendetta was against the churches, especially the pastors. After all, the story of Egyptian slavery, Babylonian captivity, the struggle of the Jews against Rome, and the eventual triumph of the Roman Catholic Church fed his worst paranoid fears. Police were ordered to attend all services. They recorded the license numbers of automobiles parked near the churches during service hours. They were particularly disturbed over sermons about Jesus standing up to the Romans. The fact that Jesus was willing to shed His blood for the people was especially offensive to the officers and their heavy-handed bosses.

Ceaușescu's move to defrock a deeply appreciated pastor in Timisoara sparked unforeseen demonstrations by unarmed believers. A bad situation was made worse when the authorities called for a mass meeting in the central park areas near downtown Bucharest. This mass meeting was supposed to be under the control of the government for the purposes of helping them get a new hold on the people. Instead, it turned out to be a hymn-singing protest in favor of the pastor and against the despotic arm of the government.

On December 22, the army discarded their weapons and started fraternizing with the protesters. On that same day, Ceauşescu and his wife, Elena, fled the presidential palace in a helicopter while a loyal aide held a gun to the head of the pilot. The pilot landed near a farmhouse after falsely affirming an antiaircraft radar beam had locked on to the helicopter. The presidential couple took off on foot, wandering aimlessly through the countryside. There were bizarre episodes, such as a car chase by citizens trying to make an arrest. Administrative aides deserted the couple. They hid for a time in an unoccupied school. The Ceauşescus, Nicolae and Elena, in one 24-hour period, lost control of Romania, the country they had considered their own. The bizarre collapse of the rulers was almost over. They were arrested and locked in a car for several hours while the police decided what to do with them.

The next day, December 25, 1989, both of the Ceauşescus were put on trial, found guilty, and executed by a firing squad. Their bodies were dragged through the streets of Bucharest. By nightfall thousands of citizens were walking the streets singing Christmas songs for the first time since President Ceauşescu had forbade them years before. Trees were decorated with Christmas ornaments. Churches were open for Christmas services without the frightening presence of the guards. Out in front of one of these churches was a homemade sign that simply read, "The Lamb Won!"

Jesus, the Lamb of God

Jesus had many titles, including Messiah, King, and Redeemer. But none of these was more descriptive than *the Lamb of God*. In near literal sense, He left heaven and came to earth to be offered as the Lamb of God who would take away the sin of the world.

Three strong statements on Jesus as the Lamb of God were spoken or written by three of the greatest followers of Jesus.

- "John [the Baptist] saw Jesus coming toward him and said, 'Look, the Lamb of God, who takes away the sin of the world!' . . . Then John gave this testimony: 'I saw the Spirit come down from heaven as a dove and remain on him . . . I have seen and I testify that this is the Son of God.' The next day John was there. . . . he said, 'Look, the Lamb of God!'" (John 1:29, 32, 34-35).

- Paul in his first letter to the Corinthians reported that Christ who had been sacrificed was "our Passover lamb" (1 Cor. 5:7).

- "Then I [John] saw a Lamb, looking as if it had been slain, standing in the center of the throne, encircled by the four living creatures and the elders. He had seven horns and seven eyes, which are the seven spirits of God sent out into all the earth. . . . And when he had taken it, the four living creatures and the twenty-four elders fell down before the Lamb. Each one had a harp and they were holding golden bowls full of incense, which are the prayers of the saints. . . . In a loud voice they sang: 'Worthy is the Lamb, who was slain, to receive power and wealth and wisdom and strength and honor and glory and praise!'" (Rev. 5:6, 8, 12).

The official high priest of the old order did not die for the sins of the people; the sacrificial lamb died or, more accurately, was slain. But in the New Testament, the faithful servant of Isa. 53 laid down His life and was thus priest and victim in one person at the same moment. The Book of John tells us several things about the death of Christ:

- Christ's sacrifice is the gift of God.
- The purpose of the Lamb's death was to take away the sin of the world.
- The death of the Lamb was the glorification of Christ.
- "No one has ever gone into heaven except the one who came from heaven—the Son of Man" (3:13).
- "But I, when I am lifted up from the earth, will draw all men to myself" (12:32).

In His magnificent prayer in John 17, Jesus said that He had glorified the Father in heaven by completing the work He had been given to do on earth. He was sent to earth to sacrifice His life or shed His blood for our salvation.

"I have brought you glory on earth by completing the work you gave me to do" (v. 4).

Paul united the purity of Christ to His sacrificial death as *a lamb without spot or blemish.*

> This righteousness from God comes through faith in Jesus Christ to all who believe. There is no difference, for all have sinned and fall short of the glory of God, and are justified freely by his grace through the redemption that came by Christ Jesus. God presented him as a sacrifice of atonement, through faith in his blood. He did this to demonstrate his . . . justice at the present time, so as to be just and the one who justifies those who have faith in Jesus *(Rom. 3:22-26).*

Several Characteristics of Christ's Sacrifice Are Included in the Letters of Paul

1. Redemption and sacrifice are just as inseparable as repentance and faith.

- "And are justified freely by his grace through the redemption that came by Christ Jesus" (Rom. 3:24).
- "It is because of him that you are in Christ Jesus, who has become for us wisdom from God—that is, our righteousness, holiness and redemption" (1 Cor. 1:30).
- "In him we have redemption through his blood, the forgiveness of sins, in accordance with the riches of God's grace . . . Who is a deposit guaranteeing our inheritance until the redemption of those who are God's possession—to the praise of his glory" (Eph. 1:7, 14).
- "For this reason Christ is the mediator of a new covenant, that those who are called may receive the promised eternal inheritance—now that he has died as a ransom to set them free from the sins committed under the first covenant" (Heb. 9:15).

2. God himself is the initiator of the sacrifice of Christ.

3. The sacrifice is described by Paul as an *expiation* (an act that makes amends) or *propitiation* (an act of reconciliation).

   - "Since we have now been justified by his blood, how much more shall we be saved from God's wrath through him!" (Rom. 5:9).
   - "And to wait for his Son from heaven, whom he raised from the dead—Jesus, who rescues us from the coming wrath" (1 Thess. 1:10).

4. Christ's sacrifice is an efficacious act on humanity's behalf.

   - "Therefore, since we have been justified through faith, we have peace with God through our Lord Jesus Christ" (Rom. 5:1).

- "God presented him as a sacrifice of atonement, through faith in his blood. He did this to demonstrate his justice, because in his forbearance he had left the sins committed beforehand unpunished" (3:25).
- "He was delivered over to death for our sins and was raised to life for our justification" (4:25).

The Blood of Christ Is a Strong Metaphor for Salvation

Approximately three dozen references to the blood of Christ are found in the New Testament. Blood and death appear in parallel passages:

- "Since we have now been justified by his blood, how much more shall we be saved from God's wrath through him! For if, when we were God's enemies, we were reconciled to him through the death of his Son, how much more, having been reconciled, shall we be saved through his life!" (Rom. 5:9-10).
- "How much more, then, will the blood of Christ, who through the eternal Spirit offered himself unblemished to God, cleanse our consciences from acts that lead to death, so that we may serve the living God!" (Heb. 9:14).

The writers of the New Testament were not interested in the blood as such, but what it stood for. The purpose of the blood was for personal salvation through the death of the Son of God. The blood of Christ is a symbol for the saving work of Christ.

The Idea of Substitution

Was Christ's death in any way a substitute for something that was due humanity? Substitution could mean that the guilty party goes completely free, relieved of the threat of punishment that he or she would otherwise have sustained. But Christ was also our representative, and as we observed earlier, this revises the idea of substitution in a way that connects us to His suffering. Nevertheless, the sacrifice of Christ did something for us that we could not do for ourselves. What the blood did is spelled out in passages like the following:

- "God made him who had no sin to be sin for us, so that in him we might become the righteousness of God" (2 Cor. 5:21).
- "Christ redeemed us from the curse of the law by becoming a curse for us" (Gal. 3:13).
- "He himself bore our sins in his body on the tree, so that we might die to sins and live for righteousness; by his wounds you have been healed" (1 Pet. 2:24).
- "For Christ died for sins once for all, the righteous for the unrighteous, to bring you to God" (3:18).

God's justice would not permit you and me to go unpunished; His judgment fell upon all sinners. But to overcome the contention between His justice and His love, He had Christ be our representative on the Cross. This didn't mean we were freed from our obligation to God. Remember the biblical idea of corporate personality—the representative and the represented share in the experiences of each other (see p. 40). But Jesus being both God and human spanned the gulf separating us from God. In this way reconciliation between God and His human creatures could be realized. Forgiveness of the sinner becomes a genuinely moral possibility, since God's honor and law are maintained. Jesus represented us in our sin to God in the same way He represented God and His forgiveness to us so we might be made righteous.

- "He poured out his life unto death, and was numbered with the transgressors. For he bore the sin of many, and made intercession for the transgressors" (Isa. 53:12).
- "So Christ was sacrificed once to take away the sins of many people; and he will appear a second time, not to bear sin, but to bring salvation to those who are waiting for him" (Heb. 9:28).

There is in the sacrifice of Christ the fact that Jesus experienced judgment as only God can experience it and our humanity was due it. This is possible because He was fully divine and fully human. He was the God-Man and therefore experienced divine love and human sin.

Reconciliation

Justification is the saving of the sinner from all guilt of sin, while *reconciliation* is the restoration of the sinner to full fellowship with God. Sin is *alienation*, which disrupts fellowship with God and introduces hostility among persons. Sin destroys the relationship between God and humanity. The work of Christ was the means for reconciling humanity with God. This is particularly taught by Paul.

- "For if, when we were God's enemies, we were reconciled to him through the death of his Son, how much more, having been reconciled, shall we be saved through his life!" (Rom. 5:10).
- "All this is from God, who reconciled us to himself through Christ and gave us the ministry of reconciliation: that God was reconciling the world to himself in Christ, not counting men's sins against them. And he has committed to us the message of reconciliation" (2 Cor. 5:18-19).
- "And through him to reconcile to himself all things,

whether things on earth or things in heaven, by making peace through his blood, shed on the cross" (Col. 1:20).

Reconciliation means a complete change in our relationship with God. We exchange one set of relationships with God for a new set. Before repentance and faith there is hostility in us because of sin. But after faith there is life, righteousness, hope, love, and peace.

Reconciliation Is the Work of God in Christ

- "God was reconciling the world to himself in Christ, not counting men's sins against them" (2 Cor. 5:19).
- "For if, when we were God's enemies, we were reconciled to him through the death of his Son, how much more, having been reconciled, shall we be saved through his life!" (Rom. 5:10).
- "By abolishing in his flesh the law with its commandments and regulations. His purpose was to create in himself one new man out of the two, thus making peace, and in this one body to reconcile both of them to God through the cross, by which he put to death their hostility" (Eph. 2:15-16).

Reconciliation initiated by the love of God has humanity as its object. It is humanity, not God, who needs to be reconciled. The sinner is helpless and thus cannot overcome the alienation between himself or herself and God. Humanity can only experience reconciliation by the act of God's love.

- "But God demonstrates his own love for us in this: While we were still sinners, Christ died for us" (Rom. 5:8).
- "For if, when we were God's enemies, we were reconciled to him through the death of his Son, how much more, having been reconciled, shall we be saved through his life!" (v. 10).

The Death of Christ and Holy Living

The death of Christ provides the forgiveness of sins (Eph. 1:7), justification (Rom. 5:9), reconciliation (v. 11; 2 Cor. 5:18), and eternal life (John 3:16; 10:10). But Christ also makes possible a clean life lived in holiness.

Sanctification is both a crisis and a process. There is initial sanctification at the time of the new birth. There is further sanctification at the time of total submission to the purpose and will of God in our lives. In our spiritual pilgrimage, there are many junctions in life where our habits, attitudes, reactions, and responses call for the sanctifying power of the Holy Spirit if we are to meet the standard for holy living indicated in the Bible. In Paul's letter to the Ephesians he made it clear that relationships in marriage and within the congregation are subject to the sanctifying work of the Holy Spirit. You can be born again and still be at odds with people in the *family* and the *congregation*.

- "Husbands, love your wives, just as Christ loved the church and gave himself up for her to make her holy, cleansing her by the washing with water through the word, and to present her to himself as a radiant church, without stain or wrinkle or any other blemish, but holy and blameless" (Eph. 5:25-27).
- "For he chose us in him before the creation of the world to be holy and blameless in his sight" (1:4).
- "Who gave himself for us to redeem us from all wickedness and to purify for himself a people that are his very own, eager to do what is good" (Titus 2:14).

Summary Statements on the Death of Christ as the Atonement for the Sins of Believers

1. Christ's death on the Cross was an objective, once-for-all, historical event.

- "Unlike the other high priests, he does not need to offer sacrifices day after day, first for his own sins, and then for the sins of the people. He sacrificed for their sins once for all when he offered himself" (Heb. 7:27).

- "He did not enter by means of the blood of goats and calves; but he entered the Most Holy Place once for all by his own blood, having obtained eternal redemption" (9:12).

- "And by that will, we have been made holy through the sacrifice of the body of Jesus Christ once for all" (10:10).

- "For Christ died for sins once for all, the righteous for the unrighteous, to bring you to God. He was put to death in the body but made alive by the Spirit" (1 Pet. 3:18).

2. The cross of Christ was initiated by God and is the profoundest expression of His love.

- "For God so loved the world that he gave his one and only Son, that whoever believes in him shall not perish but have eternal life" (John 3:16).

- "Therefore, brothers, we have an obligation . . . to live according to it" (Rom. 8:12).

3. Christ died for us when we were helpless, ungodly sinners.

- "You see, at just the right time, when we were still powerless, Christ died for the ungodly. . . . But God demonstrates his own love for us in this: While we were still sinners, Christ died for us. . . . For if, when we were God's enemies, we were reconciled to him through the death of his Son, how much more, having been reconciled, shall we be saved through his life!" (Rom. 5:6, 8, 10).

- "This is love: not that we loved God, but that he loved us and sent his Son as an atoning sacrifice for our sins" (1 John 4:10).

4. The sign of the Cross is the sign of victory. Through the sacrifice of Christ, God dealt a decisive blow to the power of evil in the world and to the power of sin and death in the lives of men and women.

   "He who does what is sinful is of the devil, because the devil has been sinning from the beginning. The reason the Son of God appeared was to destroy the devil's work" (1 John 3:8).

5. The Cross means deliverance from the guilt and power of sin.
   - "Who gave himself for us to redeem us from all wickedness and to purify for himself a people that are his very own, eager to do what is good" (Titus 2:14).
   - "God made him who had no sin to be sin for us, so that in him we might become the righteousness of God" (2 Cor. 5:21).
   - "Christ redeemed us from the curse of the law by becoming a curse for us" (Gal. 3:13).

The Lamb won, but before we can be fully saved, our own responsibilities will be discussed in the next chapter.

Talking Points

- In what ways did Jesus become the Lamb of God?
- How does John the Baptist fit into the concept of Jesus as the Lamb of God?
- What was the role of the lamb in the ancient celebration of the atonement?
- How did the Lamb win in Romania's rebellion?
- As God's Lamb, how was Jesus without spot or blemish?

5

HOW CAN I BE SAVED?

THE PHARISEE AND THE PUBLICAN

Two men went up into the temple to pray;
the one a Pharisee,
and the other a publican.
The Pharisee stood and prayed thus
with himself,
God, I thank thee,
that I am not as other men are,
extortioners, unjust, adulterers,
or even as this publican.
I fast twice in the week,
I give tithes of all that I possess.
Luke 18:10-12, KJV

✱ ✱ ✱

DEEPER THAN THE STAIN HAS GONE

Dark the stain that soiled man's nature,
Long the distance that he fell,
Far removed from hope and heaven,
Into deep despair and hell.
But there was a fountain opened,
And the blood of God's own Son,
Purifies the soul and reaches
Deeper than the stain has gone.
—Adger McDavid Pace, 1882—1959

✱ ✱ ✱

I had just left the pro shop and was walking across the broad porch that sheltered the doorway of the golf shop when my friend said, "I didn't see Fred in there this morning; did you?"

"I sure didn't," I replied. "You wait here. I'm going back and see if Fred is around." I turned on my heel and went back to inquire about Fred. His assistant behind the desk said, "Oh, haven't you heard? Fred is in the hospital with terminal cancer." He continued talking, trying to find ways to soften the news. But *terminal cancer* has a feeling of dread from which more words cannot detract.

To understand this story, you need to know who Fred was. Fred Lawson was the best-known and most popular man in our city of several hundred thousand. He was more popular than the general manager of Buick or Chevrolet, the two businesses that dominated our local economy. Fred not only ran a high quality municipal golf course in the summer but also taught golf to the junior high and high school students during the school year. Everybody knew him, and to know Fred was to like him. Just to demonstrate his popularity, the city sponsored a Fred Lawson Day!

All the businessmen's clubs, like Rotary and Kiwanis, got their members to volunteer to stand at certain intersections with buckets in hand for drivers to give toward a trip for Fred and his wife back to Scotland. If enough money came in, the city was going to send him home. With his wife, he was going back to the place of his birth and the Scottish course where he first learned to play golf. Enough money was received in the buckets in one day to pay for the entire trip plus a generous purse of walk-around money. It was a magnificent show of love and appreciation from a city to someone they wanted to honor.

But back to the story: When I returned from the pro shop to the porch, I reported to my friend that Fred had the dreaded disease of cancer. We stood quietly for a few moments. Then I said softly, almost to myself, "I wonder if he is saved." Then I continued with a stronger voice, "Oh, I suppose he's a member of the First Presbyterian Church." That was the largest and most distinguished congregation in town. "I'm sure Dr. Mullenau will call on him. Most of the leading citizens in our city are members of his church. I would guess that Fred and his wife go there."

This little self-conversation was intended to get me off the spot and make it the responsibility of someone else to be concerned with the eternal soul of Fred Lawson. It frightened me to think about going to the 12-story hospital in our community to talk with Fred. It especially intimidated me to think about trying to find out if he were saved.

I went home from the golf course. My wife, Lora Lee, and I had lunch in the kitchen of the parsonage. But I couldn't get Fred out of my mind. Fred might need to be saved. I didn't think that way about other people who got cancer, but with Fred, things were different. I could not get his salvation out of my mind! And if I didn't do anything about it, I was going to feel more and more guilty for longer than I wanted to.

I thought about Fred Lawson the rest of the day and picked up on my concern the next morning. After lunch, Lora Lee and I backed out of the driveway in our Buick, the only car for our town. But I turned the wrong direction, away from the place we said we were going. In her inimitable way, Lora Lee said, "It is going to be about 25,000 miles around the way you are headed. It was then I told her what I intended to do. I was going over to Hurley Hospital. I wanted her to stay in the car and pray. I was going up to see Fred Lawson and find out if he was ready to die.

On the way down the hall to his room, I prayed that he might be in a private room. That would make it easier to talk with him about his soul without others listening. But it didn't work out that way. He was in a four-bed room with three other men.

Fred greeted me warmly. Then we talked about everything I could think of, including the trip to Scotland, the condition of the greens on the course he supervised, and who his doctor was. We talked about how many children had been taught their golf swing by him. Finally the time was at hand. I could not stall any longer. I said quietly, "Fred, I have come for a specific reason today. I hope you get well and teach golf for years and years. But I just need to ask you a question. I don't want to put you down or embarrass you, but I need to know something. Are you ready to die because you know Jesus Christ as your personal Savior?" It seemed to me every man in the room came up on his elbow to hear better. But Fred also raised himself up. He extended his hand. Then he began weeping so profusely the bed began to shake visibly. He grasped my hand in both of his. He had the powerful hands of a professional golfer. Then he said, "No! I don't know if I am a Christian. I do know I am not ready to die."

I began to explain to him the major steps to salvation. (1) Do you realize you are a sinner who needs help? (2) Do you realize you cannot earn your salvation by your good works? (3) Do you realize salvation comes only through the atonement of Jesus Christ? (4) Are you ready to repent of your sins and believe in the grace of God that comes through Christ?

I explained each one of these four questions, reviewed some verses to match them, and gave him time for questions. When we finished, we had a wonderful prayer together. He squeezed my hand again as it hadn't been squeezed in a long time, if ever. And I said good-bye. But before he let me go, he said, "Several ministers have been here to see me, but you are the only one who has asked me if I am saved. Thank you! Thank you!"

Fred Lawson went home from the hospital to die. I called on him at least once each week. I never visited him that he did not thank me again for the hospital visit that brought him the truth of salvation and led him to a saving knowledge of Christ. Mrs. Lawson told me he never had a visitor—and he had visits from the best known people in town—without telling them the story of my visit to his room in Hurley Hospital where he received God's gift of salvation.

One Sunday, the telephone was ringing as we came into the house from church. It was Mrs. Lawson. She said Fred had just gone to be with the Lord, only moments before she called. Could I please come for the family's sake? While waiting for the mortician, I sat with the family while Mrs. Lawson told me the story of his passing. She said, "He seemed to know the end was at hand. He asked me to bring all the family into the bedroom, which I did.

Then," she said, "Fred had something personal to say to each member of the family. Then he told the family one more time about my visit to his hospital room and his own assurance of salvation. And after that," she said, "he turned his face to the wall and was gone."

In the rest of this chapter, we will look at the four steps to eternal life I gave to Fred Lawson and the partial list of scriptures on which they rest.

1. Realize You Are a Sinner Who Needs Help

Among the many sayings in the Bible that underscore the sinfulness of our nature, here are three—two from the pen of Paul and one from the writings of the prophet Jeremiah:

- Rom. 5:12: "Therefore, just as sin entered the world through one man, and death through sin, and in this way death came to all men, *because all sinned*" (emphasis added).
- Jer. 17:9-10: "*The heart is deceitful* above all things and beyond cure. Who can understand it? I the LORD search the heart and examine the mind" (emphasis added).
- Rom. 6:23: "For the *wages of sin is death,* but the gift of God is eternal life in Christ Jesus our Lord" (emphasis added).

There are three kinds of people who feel no need for salvation: (1) the arrogant, (2) the misinformed, and (3) the spiritually infirm.

The *arrogant sinner* is often one who sees himself or herself superior to others because of social status, educational achievement, or good works.

In an effort to teach the importance of spiritual humility, Jesus told the people a parable, a very intriguing story with a powerful application. Luke says the story was addressed "to some who were confident of their *own righteousness* and *looked down* on everybody else" (Luke 18:9, emphasis added).

According to Jesus, "two men went up to the temple to pray, one a Pharisee and the other a tax collector" (v. 10). These two categories, within the population of Palestine, were the cultural extremes in social status, educational status, and good works. In these matters, the Pharisees were head and shoulders above the despised tax collectors.

What Is a Pharisee?

The roots of the Pharisees, as a movement, went back 200 years before Christ when the influence of the Greeks in Palestine was so strong that many Jews shared Greek values, living more like Gentiles than pious men of the Law. The Pharisees were a reaction against the Greek influence that impacted the Mediterranean world. They served on the Sanhedrin, which was the supreme court of their day. They were spiritually arrogant, socially superior, and the supreme example of people whose salvation faith depended on a meticulous keeping of the Law. The following characteristics must be included in any profile of the Pharisees:

- The Pharisees were known for their religious practices. They fasted two days each week. They gave alms in public places while the trumpets were blown, thus assuring their continued reputation as doers of their faith.
- They were well known for supporting and observing the time-honored customs called "the tradition of the elders" (Mark 7:3).
- They observed the laws other people were less careful in keeping, such as tithing and ritual purity (Acts 26:5). They washed their hands on all ritually appropriate occasions and paid tithes on all their increase.
- They were known for strict interpretation of the Law

and its observance, especially (1) in keeping the Sabbath holy (Mark 2:24), (2) observing the divorce laws (10:2), and (3) personal honesty (Matt. 23:16-23).

- The Pharisees would not associate with Gentiles or eat in their homes. After all, the Pharisees were known as *the separated ones*.
- They believed in the resurrection of the dead, which the Sadducees did not (Acts 23:6-9).
- A Pharisee was someone who was always ready to criticize others who did not share his strict views on how the Law was to be kept.
- The Pharisees kept the Law meticulously, as far as appearances were concerned, but their hearts were often far away.
- Their motives were wrong because they wanted the praise and approval of others (Matt. 6:2, 5, 16; 23:5-7).
- According to Luke, "they trusted in *themselves* that they were righteous" (Luke 18:9, KJV, emphasis added).
- Minor details of the Law became major preoccupations with the Pharisees, while they forgot the most important matters of the Law.
- Because of the great distance between their heads and their hearts, the Pharisees were often called *hypocrites*. Jesus scolded them with sharp words: "Woe to you, teachers of the law and *Pharisees*, you *hypocrites!* You devour widows' houses and for a show make lengthy prayers. Therefore you will be *punished* more severely" (Matt. 23:14, emphasis added).

What Is a Tax Collector or Publican?

A tax collector or publican did not have a chance against a well-trained, disciplined, strong-willed Pharisee with a harsh tongue.

After all, a tax collector was a lowly, unpopular contract worker who collected taxes for the government, usually working for a publican who had a lucrative business as the chief agent in charge of an office where everyone was forced to pay up.

When taxes were discussed, anger often surged to the surface for two reasons: (1) Both the publicans and the tax collectors were mercenaries who worked for officials given to oppressing the Jews. (2) They were also hated because of the way their contracts were structured. They committed themselves to collect a certain amount of money, but with the legal right to keep for themselves anything collected above the contractual amount. The excess was theirs. So both the publicans and the tax collectors who worked for them set the tax rate at the highest amount the market would bear, often on an individual basis.

Jesus and the Rejected Classes

However, Jesus set a new precedent among the Jews by accepting and associating with these despised social rejects, tax collectors and publicans. He ate with tax collectors (Mark 2:16). He bestowed His saving grace upon them (Luke 19:9). He even chose a tax collector, Matthew, as a member of His inner group of 12. Jesus rejected the Pharisees but loved sinners, even tax collectors and publicans who realized they needed help (Matt. 9:11-14; Luke 18:10).

2. Realize You Cannot Save Yourself

Our problems of self-justification are futile for several reasons: (1) On the scale of goodness, which runs from 1 to 100, we all fail someplace. No one is perfect. (2) Even if we gave God everything we own, it would not be enough. God wants our heart, soul, mind, and strength. He also wants us to love our neighbor with the same self-serving love we bestow upon ourselves. That is more than a mortal can do!

But anything less does not fulfill the Law. (3) None of us does enough good works to deserve our salvation. In striving for perfection, it is good to be reminded by James, the brother of our Lord and bishop of the Jerusalem Church, "To him who *knows* to do good and does *not do it*, to him it is *sin* (James 4:17, NKJV, emphasis added). Moral failure is written in the mind of every mortal because we all know to do better than we do.

There are at least two great sayings, one in the Old Testament and the other in the New, that undergird the fact that we cannot earn our salvation.

- Isa. 64:6: "All of us have become like one who is unclean, and all our righteous acts are like *filthy rags;* we all *shrivel up like a leaf,* and like the wind our sins sweep us away" (emphasis added).

- Gal. 2:16: "So we, too, have put our faith in Christ Jesus that we may be *justified by faith* in Christ and not by observing the law, because by observing the law no one will be justified" (emphasis added).

3. Christ Is the Only Door to Salvation

Church membership, baptism, the Lord's Supper, and attending Sunday School are all means of grace. But none of these is the door to salvation. That door is Jesus. He said, "I am the way and the truth and the life. No one comes to the Father except *through me*" (John 14:6, emphasis added).

Peter, who fished, ate, talked, and prayed with Jesus as much, if not more, than any other man, had this to say about the role of Jesus in our salvation: "Christ also . . . suffered for sins, the just for the unjust, *that he might bring us* to God" (1 Pet. 3:18, KJV, emphasis added).

Paul set the example of spiritual self-deprecation by

highlighting his own personal unworthiness for salvation. In a letter to Timothy, his son in the faith, he repeated the essence of what he had said or written in other places at other times:

> Here is a trustworthy saying that deserves full acceptance: Christ Jesus came into the world **to save** sinners—of whom I am the *worst*. But for that very reason I was shown *mercy* so that in me, the worst of sinners, Christ Jesus might display his *unlimited patience* as an example for those who would believe on him and receive *eternal life (1 Tim. 1:15-16, emphasis added).*

In today's *New York Times,* of all places, David Brooks, a Jewish columnist, quotes John R. Stott on the revelation of truth. Stott, a London pastor, is the man some say would be pope if evangelicals had one. He is accorded the status of diplomat, not politician, in the world where Christian faith needs defending. Our problem among secular fundamentalists "is not because we are ultra-conservative . . . or reactionary, or all the other horrid things we are sometimes said to be. It is rather because we *love Jesus Christ* and we are determined, God helping us, to bear witness to his *unique glory* and *absolute sufficiency.* In Christ and in biblical witness to Christ, God's revelation is complete. To add any words of our own to *his finished work* is derogatory to Christ" (*New York Times,* November 30, 2004).

That's the way I see it! Christ is the only door to salvation. To all those who want to be saved, knock, open, and enter!

4. Repent and Be Baptized

Peter was the choice of Christ for preacher on Pentecost Sunday. This was the day when the Holy Spirit was poured out on believers and "about three thousand were added to their number that day" (Acts 2:41). There are several interesting observations on this Sunday morning service in the outer court of the Jerusalem Temple.

Peter was not a hit-and-run celebrity who was invited in for the grand launching of a new church. Many of these people knew him well. Although he had a fishing business in Galilee, he had spent time in the city. He was a familiar figure to many of them, and they were people he both knew and understood.

- "Then Peter . . . raised his voice and addressed the crowd: 'Fellow Jews and all of you who live in Jerusalem, let me explain this to you; listen carefully to what I say'" (Acts 2:14).

- Even as a preacher, Peter was not a loner. Luke says, "Peter stood up with the Eleven" (v. 14). He was the designated spokesman for a group sermon. What he preached, they all believed. Other disciples might not have been as forceful and articulate as Peter, but in their own way, each of them would have covered the same subject matter if they were the chosen speaker for the day.

- The focus of Peter's sermon was Jesus, crucified, resurrected, and rejected. Of all the sermons in the Book of Acts, each of them follows the pattern Peter used on the Sunday the Church was born.

This same focus on Jesus was central in the preaching of Paul:

- "When I came to you, brothers, . . . I resolved to know nothing while I was with you except *Jesus Christ and him crucified.* I came to you in weakness and fear, and with much trembling. My *message and my preaching* were not with wise and persuasive words, but with a demonstration of the Spirit's power, so that your faith might not rest on men's wisdom, but on God's power" (1 Cor. 2:1-5, emphasis added).

Finally, Peter ended his sermon with an evangelistic appeal.

- "With many other words he *warned* them; and he *pleaded* with them, 'Save yourselves from this corrupt generation.' Those who *accepted* his message were *baptized*, and about three thousand were *added* to their number that day" (Acts 2:40-41, emphasis added).

My First Airplane Ride

I will always remember the first ride I ever had in an airplane. My father had to make a quick trip from St. Louis to Oklahoma City, down and back. He chartered a plane for his purpose, and he invited me to go with him. I was both overjoyed and scared. After all, I had never been close to a plane before, and this was 1937.

When we got to the airport, I assumed, wrongly, there would be time enough for me to examine the plane inside and out. No such luck! When we arrived, the pilot had the plane warmed up and ready to go. I didn't even have time to circle it once. After the exchange of greetings, the pilot just said, "Let's get aboard. We are ready to go." My apoplexy indicator was rising.

Once on board, things got even more scary for me. The pilot looked over his right shoulder and said loudly, "Be sure you have your safety belts fastened. It's the law!" I didn't really care if it was the law or not. I immediately began to ask myself questions about why they would have safety belts if there were not problems in the first place. I quickly concluded there must be some special danger. But I fastened my belt dutifully and carefully.

Then the pilot said something else that set my nerves on edge. He looked back over his shoulder again and said, "If you don't mind, I always like to pray before we take off." Now I believe in prayer and I am sure I would have prayed whether he did or not. But again, his call for prayer made me wonder if there were some special danger in the flight before us. After all, we did not stop to pray when we took trips in our car. Even that morning, my father did not pray when he backed our Buick out of the driveway and headed for the airport.

But finally we were tucked in, secured, and prayed for. The pilot revved up the engines until they roared. He then pulled back on whatever it is they pull back on, and the plane began to move down the ribbon of concrete. I could see out ahead to the end of the runway. I was just sure we were going to hit the fence and house and barn at the end of the airport. It was high time for me to begin helping.

I pulled up on that seatbelt for all I was worth. But nothing happened. We were just gliding along firmly over the concrete. I pulled harder; but nothing happened except we were getting closer and closer to the fence, house, and barn. Finally, I poured all my human strength into a last great big "ugh." If it were possible, I was going to lift that plane off the ground. But just then, the plane began to rise; I had finally lifted the plane off the ground and we were sailing through the clear blue sky.

All of this story is true except for one bit of misinformation. I did not lift the plane off the ground; the plane lifted me!

This flight occurred when I was only 15 years of age. But from this experience I learned a great spiritual lesson about what it means to be saved. Our strict living may be like a safety belt, but it will not lift us from the mire of sin.

Our good works may make it easier to pray. But Christ alone can save us. He will save us for this life and the next! Someday, at the end time, He will lift us to heaven on the wings of His glory and we shall live forever with the believers who also know Christ as their Savior. We will join the heavenly choir John saw and heard from the Island of Patmos on a Sunday morning when he, as a political prisoner, had no church to attend.

In a loud voice they sang:

"Worthy is the Lamb, who was slain,
to receive *power* and *wealth* and *wisdom*
and *strength*
and *honor* and *glory* and *praise!"*
(Rev. 5:12, emphasis added)

Talking Points

- What were the unique characteristics of the Pharisees and publicans?
- Why are sinners in need of help?
- In what way is Jesus the only door to heaven?
- How does a sinner accept the grace of God given through Jesus Christ?
- What assurances do we have in salvation?

6

FAITH, REPENTANCE, AND RESTITUTION

FAITH DEFINED

Now faith is being sure of what we hope for
and certain of what we do not see.
This is what the ancients were commended for.
By faith we understand that
the universe was formed at God's command,
so that what is seen
was not made out of what was visible.
Heb. 11:1-3

✱ ✱ ✱

DAVID'S REMORSE

Have mercy on me, O God,
according to your unfailing love;
according to your great compassion
blot out my transgressions.
Wash away all my iniquity
and cleanse me from my sin.
For I know my transgressions,
and my sin is always before me.
Against you, you only, have I sinned
and done what is evil in your sight,
so that you are proved right when you speak
and justified when you judge.
Surely I was sinful at birth,
sinful from the time my mother conceived me.
Ps. 51:1-5

✳ ✳ ✳

Faith looks to the future. *Repentance* faces the here and now. *Restitution* clears up the past.

In our church, the altar was the royal road to salvation. To eliminate the altar from my spiritual heritage would be like taking Wesley's hymns out of the songbook or the Gospels out of the Bible.

I knew that the Catholic Church had a different kind of altar from ours. But they were different in lots of other ways too. My best friend in school was the son of a Baptist pastor who had a special room in their church where seekers gathered in semiprivacy with spiritual counselors. I interpreted this plan as a lack of courage to pray for salvation at a public altar.

Then I made a trip to England, to the New Room chapel in Bristol where John Wesley preached during the 18th-century revival that shook the nation spiritually. It gave America its largest denomination. And according to the historians, the Wesleyan Revival saved England from a bloody revolution like the one that was about to occur in France. Because of my fixation on the altar in our church, I wanted to see the altar where Wesley's converts were saved.

It was shocking to me to see that Wesley did not have an altar, not even a Communion rail. I thought it might have been sent out for repairs or to be refinished, but I ultimately learned Wesley's altar was not there because it had never existed. I couldn't believe what I was seeing.

I sought out the sexton—the man in charge of the property—and asked him about the lack of an altar. He confirmed what I had learned from another visitor. There truly was no altar, ever. "Mr. Wesley did not use an altar like you Americans," he said with an expression just short of a smirk.

Then I said—setting myself up for a real English put-down—"Then what did he do to get people saved?" Answering me as he turned away in a show of disgust, the sexton said, "I guess Mr. Wesley just depended on the Holy Spirit."

The sexton was right. And so was John Wesley. Whether we kneel at the altar, meet with spiritual counselors in a classroom of the church, talk across a luncheon table with a friend, or kneel by the sofa in our living room, the Holy Spirit is the Agent of God the Father and His only Son, Jesus Christ, bringing men and women to salvation.

The Holy Spirit uses three roads that converge in personal salvation: (1) The main road is *faith*, the gift of God "lest any man should boast" (Eph. 2:9, KJV). (2) The super road—the interstate highway—is *repentance*, essential for a changed life. (3) And the hardest road of all is *restitution*, a narrow, bumpy road that is both theologically sound and psychologically difficult. Together, these three roads lead to the city of hope where the fulfilling emotion is joy and the most cherished possession is eternal life.

The Highway of Faith

According to the Bible, faith alone is the first condition for salvation. People have spent at least 2,000 years and unlimited psychic energy working on ways to complicate the process and confuse the meaning of salvation. Some of the issues that have been worked into the salvation formula include dietary rules, tithing, designated worship days, church membership, style of baptism, church attendance, technical theological affirmations, good works, and style of worship. And there are even more. These rules are called the oral law.

Paul wrote about a wide variety of these religious issues. But when it came to salvation, the road he identified was straight and plain. Paul agreed with Isaiah, who believed that even a fool would not get lost on this highway.

"And an *highway* shall be there, and a way, and it shall be called The way of holiness; the unclean shall not pass over it; but it shall be for those: the wayfaring men, though *fools*, shall not err therein" (Isa. 35:8, KJV, emphasis added).

For approximately two years in Ephesus, Paul had an evangelistic outreach program scheduled each afternoon in a teaching center next door to the synagogue. His work was so successful, "All the Jews and Greeks . . . in the province of Asia [modern Turkey] heard the word of the Lord" (Acts 19:10).

In a letter to these new Christians, Paul wrote, "For it is by *grace* you have been saved, through *faith*—and this not from yourselves, it is the *gift of God*—not by works, so that no one can boast" (Eph. 2:8-9, emphasis added).

When the warden of the prison in Philippi realized the tragic mistake he had made by brutalizing Paul and Silas in his dungeon, he came running in the dark. The dust from an earthquake was still trying to settle.

"The jailer called for lights, rushed in and fell trembling before Paul and Silas. He then brought them out and asked, 'Sirs, *what must I do to be saved?'* They [Paul and Silas] replied, *'Believe* in the Lord Jesus, and you will be *saved*—you and your household'" (Acts 16:29-31, emphasis added).

However, faith is also inseparably bound up with repentance. Without some measure of faith, no one can truly repent. There can be no saving faith without moving ahead on the royal highway of repentance.

What Is Faith?

It is strange that the Bible does not make any effort to explain some of its great proclamations. For instance, the Bible makes no effort to define God. The opening sentence of Genesis is a simple proclamation, "In the beginning God . . ." Nowhere in the entire Bible is there an effort to either define or defend God's existence. God is! The Scriptures move forward on that assumption.

The same is true of faith. Abraham, Moses, David, Paul, John, and all the other 37 writers of the Scriptures who talk about faith don't explain it. The nearest thing we have to an operational definition of faith is made by the unknown writer of Hebrews: "Now faith is the *substance* of things hoped for, the *evidence* of things not seen" (11:1, KJV, emphasis added).

Here is my private explanation of this affirmation about faith: *First* of all, faith is the ability to create a mental picture of what is hoped for. *Second,* faith is the ability to start acting on the mental picture, just as though it were already reality. But even that explanation of faith focuses on achieving faith, not saving faith.

Here are some leads on what faith is:

1. Faith is the bridge that connects sinful humanity with a righteous God. That bridge is Christ, provided by God's grace. This faith connector is the means by which we are justified.

   - "Know that a man is not justified by observing the law, but by *faith* in Jesus Christ. So we, too, have put our faith in Christ Jesus that we may be *justified* by faith in Christ and not by observing the law, because by observing the law no one will be justified" (Gal. 2:16, emphasis added).

   - "So the law was put in charge to lead us to Christ that we might be *justified by faith*" (3:24, emphasis added).

2. Faith is in the merits of Christ, not in the points we have earned by keeping the laws of God. "Though you have not seen him, you *love* him; and even though you do not see him now, you *believe* in him and are filled with an inexpressible and glorious joy" (1 Pet. 1:8, emphasis added).

3. Good works are the natural outgrowth of saving faith. Faith without works is no faith at all.

   What good is it, my brothers, if a man claims to have faith but has no deeds? *Can such faith save him?* Suppose a brother or sister is without clothes and daily food. If one of you says to him, "Go, I wish you well; keep warm and well fed," but does nothing about his physical needs, what good is it? In the same way, *faith* by itself, if it is not accompanied by *action*, is dead. But someone will say, "You have faith; I have deeds." Show me your faith without deeds, and I will show you my *faith by what I do*. You believe that there is one God. Good! Even the demons believe that—and shudder. You foolish man, do you want evidence that faith without deeds is useless? Was not our ancestor Abraham considered righteous for what he did when he offered his son Isaac on the altar? You see that his faith and his actions were working together, and his faith was made complete by what he did (*James 2:14-22, emphasis added*).

4. Faith is simply accepting God's Word as true. "God has given us eternal life, and this life is in his Son. He who has the Son has life; he who does not have the Son of God does not have life" (1 John 5:11-12).

5. Faith is the bridge by which our sin is *imputed* to Him and God's grace is *imparted* to us.
   - "That God was *reconciling* the world to himself in Christ, not counting men's sins against them. . . . We implore you on Christ's behalf: *Be reconciled* to God. God made him who had no sin to be sin for us, so that in him we might become the righteousness of God" (2 Cor. 5:19-21, emphasis added).
   - "It is because of him that you are in Christ Jesus, who has become for us wisdom from God—that is, *our righteousness, holiness and redemption*" (1 Cor. 1:30, emphasis added).

6. Faith covers various levels of personal commitment.
   - There can be intellectual agreement to truth without saving faith.
     —"You believe that there is one God. Good! Even the demons believe that—and shudder"

(James 2:19). They are not saved by this level or kind of belief.

- Saving faith is a personal commitment to Christ, relying on His finished work and not on Him as a prophet, wise man, or leader, but a Savior.

  —"That is why I [Paul] am suffering as I am. Yet I am not ashamed, because I *know* whom I have believed, and am *convinced* that he is able to guard what I have *entrusted* to him for that day" (2 Tim. 1:12, emphasis added).

7. Faith is the *commitment* by which salvation is received. "For by *grace* are ye saved through *faith*; and that not of yourselves: it is the *gift* of God: not of works, lest any man should boast" (Eph. 2:8-9, KJV, emphasis added). Good works flow out of saving faith.

Repentance

In the ancient world of the Greeks, repentance stood for a "change" of mind. It was a feeling of remorse and regret for bad conduct. Judas had remorse over what he did to Jesus.

"When Judas, who had betrayed him, saw that Jesus was condemned, he was seized with *remorse* and returned the thirty silver coins to the chief priests and the elders" (Matt. 27:3, emphasis added).

Repentance is an act of turning around and going in the opposite direction. This kind of spiritual repentance leads to forgiveness and a personal relationship with God. It is a fundamental and thorough change in the heart from the preoccupation with sin to the acceptance of the Lordship of Christ over your life.

In the Old Testament, the classic case of repentance

was that of King David, faced with Nathan the prophet, who accused him of killing Uriah the Hittite and committing adultery with Uriah's wife, Bathsheba. David's prayer of repentance is in Ps. 51.

In the New Testament, the keynote of repentance is sounded by John the Baptist, who cried out to the people who attended his baptisms along the Jordan,

- "Repent, for the kingdom of heaven is near" (Matt. 3:2).
- "Produce fruit in keeping with repentance" (v. 8).

After John the Baptist was imprisoned, Jesus moved to Capernaum. He used John's message of repentance and expanded it to include the good news of the gospel.

"When Jesus heard that John had been put in prison, he returned to Galilee. Leaving Nazareth, he went and lived in Capernaum. . . . From that time on Jesus began to preach, 'Repent, for the kingdom of heaven is near'" (4:12-13, 17; see also Mark 1:15).

Repentance is bound up with faith and is inseparable from it. Repentance is a turning away from the sin of disobedience and rebellion.

Essential Elements of Repentance

1. Repentance is a genuine sorrow toward God on account of sin.

    - "Even if I caused you sorrow . . . yet now I am happy, not because you were made sorry, but because your *sorrow led you to repentance*. . . . Godly sorrow brings repentance that leads to salvation" (2 Cor. 7:8-10, emphasis added).
    - "Have mercy on me, O God, according to your unfailing love; according to your great compassion blot out my transgressions" (Ps. 51:1).

2. Repentance is an inner repugnance to sin that results in the forsaking of it.
   - "Produce fruit in keeping with repentance" (Matt. 3:8).
   - "First to those in Damascus, then to those in Jerusalem and in all Judea, and to the Gentiles also, I *preached* that they should *repent* and turn to God and *prove* their repentance by their deeds" (Acts 26:20, emphasis added).
   - "Therefore let us leave the elementary teachings about Christ and go on to maturity, not laying again the foundation of repentance from acts that lead to death, and of faith in God" (Heb. 6:1).

3. Repentance is a humble self-surrender to the will and service of God. "'I am Jesus, whom you are persecuting,' he replied. 'Now get up and go into the city, and you will be told *what you must do*'" (Acts 9:5-6, emphasis added).

4. Repentance contains different stages of development:
   - The lowest and most imperfect form of repentance may arise from fear of consequence, or even sorrow over being caught.
   - Repentance deepens with the recognition of the awfulness of sin, including the hurt it does.
   - It becomes more complete and powerful in those who have experienced the enormity of sin and the depths of the compassion of God.

5. Repentance is the gift of God.
   - "God exalted him to his own right hand as Prince and Savior that he might give repentance and forgiveness of sins to Israel" (5:31).
   - "When they heard this, they had no further objections and praised God, saying, 'So then, God has

granted even the Gentiles repentance unto life'"
(11:18).

- "Or do you show contempt for the riches of his
  kindness, tolerance and patience, not realizing
  that God's kindness leads you toward repentance?"
  (Rom. 2:4).

6. Although it is left to each person to make his or her
   own decision, it is the Holy Spirit who awakens the
   conscience and leads men and women into repentance.

7. Repentance and faith are opposite sides of the same
   coin. You can't have one without the other. By repentance we turn away from sin; and in faith we turn toward God.

   - On the negative side of repentance we hear Jesus
     say, "Unless you *repent* you will all likewise *perish*"
     (Luke 13:3, NKJV, emphasis added).

   - "I tell you, no! But unless you repent, you too will
     all perish. Or those eighteen who died when the
     tower in Siloam fell on them—do you think they
     were more guilty than all the others living in Jeru-
     salem? I tell you, no! But unless you *repent*, you
     too will all *perish*" (vv. 3-5, emphasis added).

   - Then on the positive side, He said, "I tell you,
     there is rejoicing in the presence of the angels of
     God over one sinner who repents" (15:10).

8. Repentance and faith were at the heart of the message
   in the Early Church.

   - In his Pentecost sermon, Peter said, "*Repent* and
     be *baptized*, every one of you, in the name of Jesus
     Christ for the forgiveness of your sins. And you
     will receive the gift of the Holy Spirit" (Acts 2:38,
     emphasis added).

- "Repent, then, and turn to God, so that your sins may be wiped out, that times of refreshing may come from the Lord" (3:19).
- "When they heard this, they had no further objections and praised God, saying, 'So then, God has granted even the *Gentiles* repentance unto life'" (11:18, emphasis added).
- "I have declared to both *Jews and Greeks* that they must turn to God in repentance and have faith in our Lord Jesus" (20:21, emphasis added).
- "First to those in Damascus, then to those in Jerusalem and in all Judea, and to the Gentiles also, I preached that they should *repent* and turn to God and *prove* their repentance by their deeds" (26:20, emphasis added).

9. Repentance is the gift of God's sovereign love.
   - "God exalted him to his own right hand as Prince and Savior that he might give repentance and forgiveness of sins to Israel" (5:31).
   - "When they heard this, they had no further objections and praised God, saying, 'So then, God has granted even the Gentiles repentance unto life'" (11:18).
   - "Or do you show contempt for the riches of his kindness, tolerance and patience, not realizing that God's kindness leads you toward repentance?" (Rom. 2:4).

Restitution

Restitution is sound not only theologically but psychologically as well. The happiest Christians are those who rejoice in God's grace and live with a sense of integrity that comes to those who have taken the time, energy, and assets to straighten out their crooked paths.

Some years ago, I was invited to be the speaker for Spiritual Emphasis Week at a Christian college in Canada. I prayed with students at the public altar and engaged in private conversations in the campus counseling room assigned me. I believe those in charge felt the effort was successful.

However, about two weeks after returning home, I got a letter from a student who told me his story. He wrote,

> I did not come forward to the altar, because I had something to do about my spiritual welfare. After the meeting closed, I borrowed money and flew home to Hamilton, Ontario, with the specific purpose of making restitution. I had two overwhelming feelings. First, I was so scared I didn't know if I could go through with my confession and offer to make things right. And second, my heart was so heavy with guilt, I thought it would break. I know part of my intention to be a minister was to get rid of guilt. If I were in the ministry, surely I would not feel this way.
>
> On the first day after arriving home, I showed up in the office of a man who had employed me for three years in high school so I could get some money for going to college. But I had betrayed his confidence. I stole unashamedly! I was a real heel!
>
> I could not keep my composure during the confession and broke out into tears. I told my former employer I wanted forgiveness if he felt he could give it. I certainly did not deserve it. But whether he forgave me or not, I told him I would make full restitution, dollar for dollar, on all I had taken.

This student's remorse was so genuine I could feel the sorrow coming through the letter.

This student's story had a glorious ending. The storeowner not only forgave him but refused the restitution money. He returned to the campus in western Canada, where he took time to send me his story in a handwritten letter.

Time marches on! Some years had gone by when I was invited to speak in a pastors and wives retreat in Winona Lake, Indiana. When I turned from the trunk of our car to carry our suitcases up the steep steps into the hotel, I saw a young man standing at the top, exuding happiness and joy. He insisted on taking our suitcases—I don't know why he didn't come to the bottom of the steps instead of waiting at the top.

Immediately he started telling me his story. He was the young man who wrote me the letter from Canada about his restitution. To say the least, he was all joy.

That night at dinner, I mentioned the young man's name and asked a generic question about the quality of his ministry. My question set off a barrage of good from all those who heard it. It was the denominational administrator who said, "That young man is at peace with God, with his congregation, with himself, and with anything else that impacts his life. I wish I had a dozen more young pastors just like him." I never did tell the group—not even the district superintendent—the restitution story. It was none of their business. But to myself, I smiled inwardly and said, "That young man is at peace with everyone and everything because he was willing to pay the full price of repentance, including the practical steps available to him for straightening up the crooked paths of the past."

Restitution for past sins is not always possible, and it is never easy. But the rewards are magnificent in their outreach and duration. They can touch any place you have ever been, any person you have ever encountered, and any situation that involved you.

Zacchaeus was a tormented man. He was so short he had to climb a tree to get a good look at the Lord. He was despised because of his business as a tax collector. He did not even know, himself, how many people he had cheated by charging them more taxes than they actually owed. He tried to compensate for the kind of person he was by living in a big house, owning many slaves, and moving around Jericho in an entourage usually saved for heads of state.

But the compensations didn't work. He was rich but miserable. In spite of his expensive trappings he was still a social reject and a turncoat who made his living from the overseas rulers in Rome. People in Jericho stayed out of his way. He was lonely and unfulfilled.

Then one day Zacchaeus met Jesus. Jesus not only treated him with respect but also invited him out of the tree for a personal conversation. He even went home with Zacchaeus for dinner. Then came the eye-opening moment; Zacchaeus promised he would make restitution for all the false taxes he had collected from the people, even up to 40 percent interest.

Courts of law make people pay restitution. But the real spiritual victory comes to the man or woman who confesses his or her sins to Christ and then talks out the situation with the very people he or she has wronged. At that point restitution is up to each penitent sinner who has received God's saving grace. What you do and how you do it is strictly a personal matter. But the happiest people on earth are those forgiven sinners who have seriously made some sort of restitution on their own.

Talking Points

- What is faith?
- What is repentance?